The Story of S

written by Pam Bishop

illustrated by Beccy Blake, Chris Brown,
John Storey and Martin Ursell

Contents

What is scurvy?

Scurvy is one of the oldest known diseases. The Egyptians suffered from scurvy-like **symptoms** over 3,000 years ago. For a very long time doctors did not know what caused scurvy or how it could be treated.

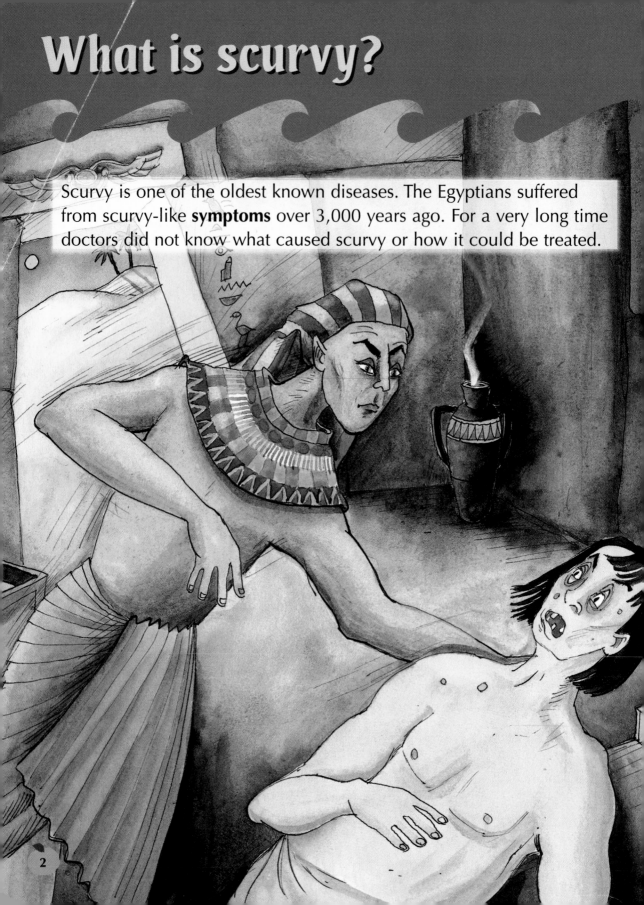

The symptoms were very dangerous:

- you got very tired
- you could not walk or eat properly
- there were sores in your mouth
- your gums would bleed and your teeth would fall out
- your legs would go purple and swell up
- it was a dangerous disease and you might die

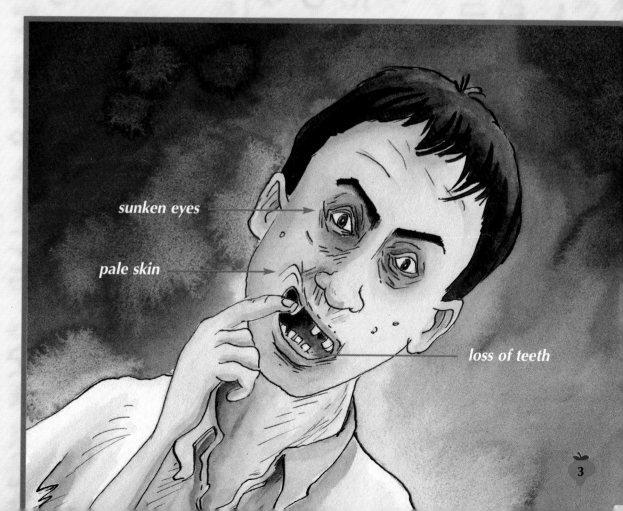

sunken eyes

pale skin

loss of teeth

Who suffered from scurvy?

In the 18 century scurvy was a very common disease amongst sailors.

British ships sailed all over the world. As they needed the wind to drive them along, the ships were at sea for a long time.

Many sailors became ill and died of scurvy while they were at sea. Nobody knew how to stop the illness or treat people who had it.

On one trip made by the Portuguese **navigator**, Vasco da Gama, about 100 of his 170 crew died on board ship.

Vasco da Gama ▲

In 1593 Sir Richard Hawkins discovered that if his crew ate oranges and lemons they did not become ill. But no one at that time picked up the idea that fruit helped stop scurvy.

Sir Richard Hawkins ▲

A clue to the disease

In the 1700s a remarkable true story gave doctors a clue about what caused the disease. Here is the story.

A sailor became very ill at sea and his legs were so swollen that he could not walk.

The captain thought other sailors might catch the disease. So he left the sailor on an island to die.

On the island, the sailor had to eat grass. Before long he was feeling better and started to move around again.

It seemed like a miracle, especially when the sailor got back to England on another ship and was able to tell his story.

SAILOR SURVIVES SCURVY

Dr Lind's idea

A Scottish surgeon called Dr James Lind was very interested in this amazing story. He was a doctor in the navy and he knew how many sailors were dying of scurvy. He began to think about the problem. One idea he had was that scurvy was caused by a germ.

▲ *Dr Lind was interested in curing scurvy because he worked with many sailors who had died from the disease.*

But he also thought that maybe there was there a link between scurvy and the grass that the sailor had eaten on the island.

He thought that perhaps scurvy had something to do with the food that the sailors were eating. This was his **hypothesis**.

Dr Lind's experiment

On 20 May 1747 Dr Lind began an experiment at sea with 12 sailors on board a ship called the *Salisbury*. The sailors all had the symptoms of scurvy.

Dr Lind divided the men into six pairs. They all had their normal food but he gave a different treatment to each group.

- Group 1 drank a mug of cider each day

- Group 2 gargled with very mild sulphuric acid

- Group 3 had two spoonfuls of vinegar, three times each day

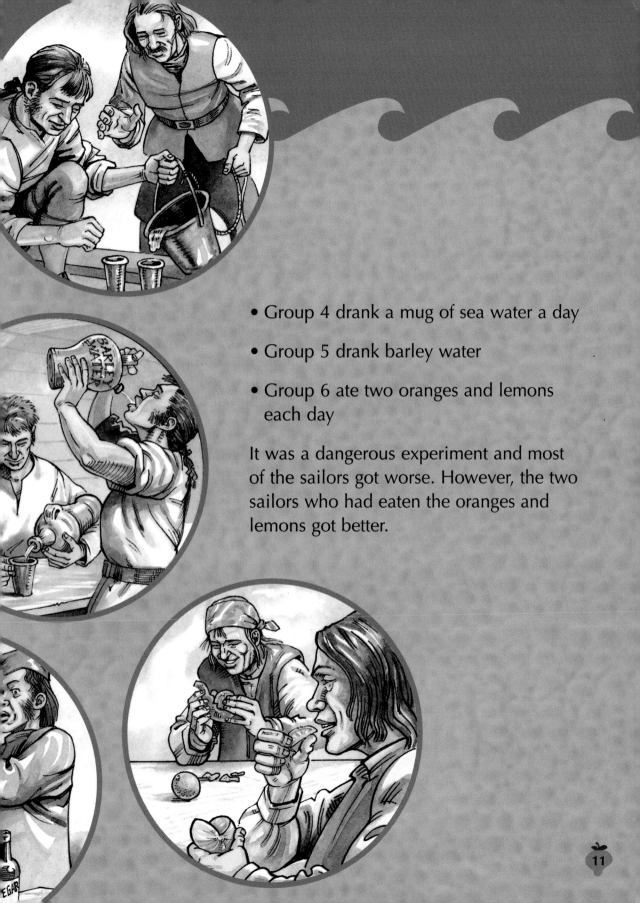

- Group 4 drank a mug of sea water a day

- Group 5 drank barley water

- Group 6 ate two oranges and lemons each day

It was a dangerous experiment and most of the sailors got worse. However, the two sailors who had eaten the oranges and lemons got better.

Dr Lind had discovered that eating fruit helped cure scurvy. But he did not know *why* his experiment had worked.

How had the fruit managed to cure the men? How did the fruit have the same effect as the fresh grass that the sailor on the island had eaten?

The answer was not discovered for another 150 years. However, Dr Lind's investigation did help to save the lives of many sailors because they took fresh fruit with them to sea.

Dr Lind worked on his ideas for about another 40 years. In 1794 he carried out another experiment. A whole fleet of ships was given enough raw lemon juice to last for 6 months. Not one sailor had scurvy in that time.

Doctors thought that the **acid** in the fruit was helping the sailors. Lime juice contains even more acid than lemons, so they thought this would work better.

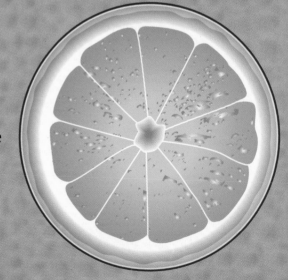

In 1795, all British sailors were told they had to drink lime juice at sea. It worked! Scurvy stopped being a problem.

British sailors are still sometimes called "limeys".

A lime a day keeps the scurvy away!

What causes disease?

In the 1800s doctors and scientists started to understand more about what caused different illnesses and how they could be treated.

Dr Jenner discovered how to vaccinate people to stop them getting smallpox. ▶

◀ *In 1854 John Snow proved that dirty water caused cholera.*

◀ *Joseph Lister carried out a knee operation using an antiseptic to stop the wound getting infected.*

But most people still thought that it was the acid in the fresh fruit that killed off germs and cured scurvy.

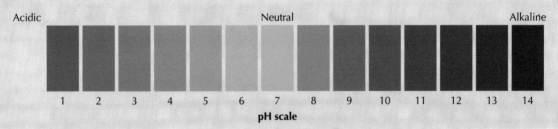

| Acidic | | | | | | Neutral | | | | | | | Alkaline |
| 1 | 2 | 3 | 4 | 5 | 6 | 7 | 8 | 9 | 10 | 11 | 12 | 13 | 14 |

pH scale

▲ *Acidity is measured by its pH value.*

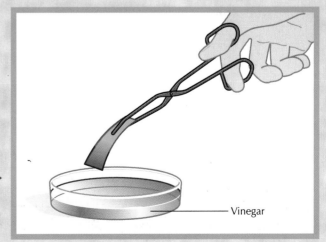

Indicator paper changes ▶ *colour to show the pH of a liquid.*

Vinegar

17

The discovery of vitamins

It was not until the beginning of the 1900s that scientists understood what Dr Lind had discovered. He had discovered the power of **vitamins**.

The Daily News

VITAMINS DISCOVERED!

The News Today

FINALLY, THE TRUTH IS OUT!

Dr Lind's experiment in 1747 was the beginning of the search for vitamins.

Scientists found that animals like mice became ill if important chemicals were missing from their **diet**. These chemicals were not needed in large amounts. They did not give the animals energy to live and grow, but they did keep them healthy and fit.

These chemicals were called vitamins.

Scientists in hospitals today working to find new cures for diseases.

Vitamin C

The vitamin which stopped scurvy was not discovered until the 1930s.

Scientists carried out experiments with lemon juice. They made a liquid from the lemons that was 20,000 times stronger than the lemon juice itself. They tested this liquid to find out what it was made of. Finally they had discovered vitamin C! (Its proper chemical name is **ascorbic acid**.)

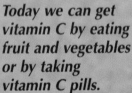

Today we can get vitamin C by eating fruit and vegetables or by taking vitamin C pills.

The scientists had found an explanation for the work that Dr Lind had done almost 200 years earlier. They also proved that illness is not always caused by infection from an attack of germs.

It is sometimes caused by a **deficiency**, or something missing, in the diet. Scurvy is a deficiency disease.

▲ *A balanced diet helps prevent deficiency diseases.*

A healthy diet

The very best foods for providing vitamin C in our diet are fresh fruit and vegetables, such as:

- oranges
- grapefruit
- blackcurrants
- kiwi
- green peppers
- potatoes
- broccoli
- lemons
- tangerines
- melons
- strawberries
- red peppers
- cabbage

Green grass is also useful – as the sailor on the island found out!

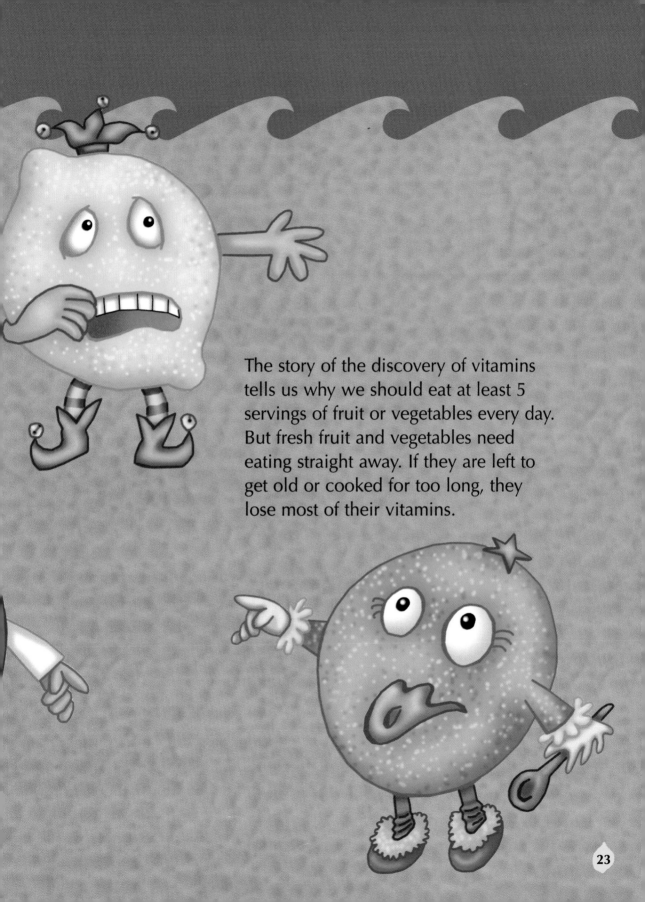

The story of the discovery of vitamins tells us why we should eat at least 5 servings of fruit or vegetables every day. But fresh fruit and vegetables need eating straight away. If they are left to get old or cooked for too long, they lose most of their vitamins.

What does vitamin C do?

What does vitamin C do in the body?

Vitamin C is important for keeping bones healthy. Without vitamin C the skeleton would not be strong. Arms and legs that are broken would be slow to mend.

Vitamin C also stops the body from catching other diseases and helps to fight off infections.

Vitamin C keeps teeth and gums healthy.

Vitamin C is needed for making **collagen** in the body. Collagen is essential for keeping bones, tendons and ligaments strong.

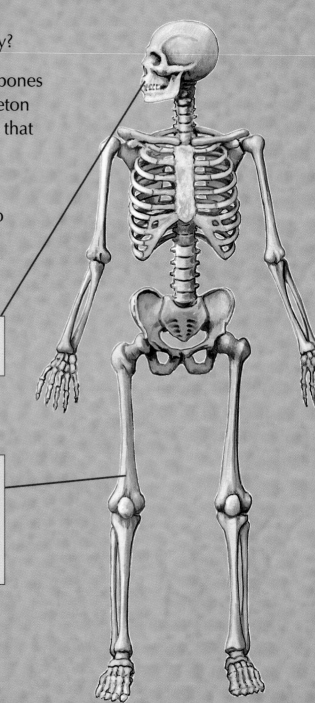

▲ *The human skeleton*

Arteries carry blood away from the heart.

The heart pumps the blood around the body.

Blood vessels and red cells in the blood need vitamin C. It helps the body to heal cuts and bruises.

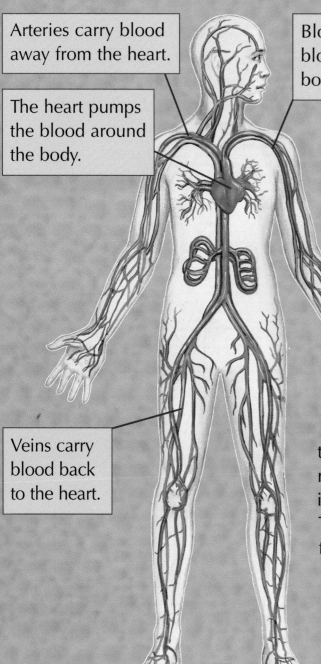

Veins carry blood back to the heart.

But ... why didn't the fresh fruit they ate at the start of the voyage stop the sailors getting scurvy?

Vitamin C is carried around in the blood. Once the body has taken what it needs the rest cannot be stored. It is passed out in urine when we go to the toilet. That is why it is important to eat foods rich in vitamin C every day.

▲ *The circulatory system*

Scurvy today

Today, babies and old people may still suffer from scurvy although it is not common. Scurvy in babies is called *Barlow's disease*. It can happen if babies are not given enough fruit juice to drink when they stop having milk from their mother.

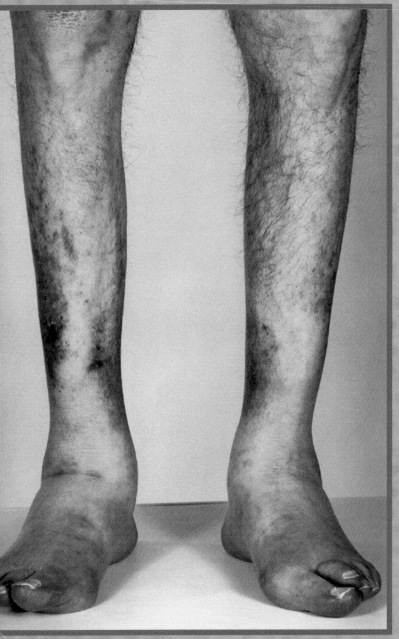

▲ *The bruised and swollen legs of a scurvy sufferer.*

A survey across America showed that over seven million American adults are in danger of getting scurvy.

Doctors have worked out how much vitamin C we should have every day. Men should have more than women. Women who are having babies need extra. About forty per cent of men and women do not have the right amount.

It is important not to worry about getting scurvy. Dr James Lind and other doctors have proved that if we eat enough fruit and vegetables we will not suffer from scurvy.

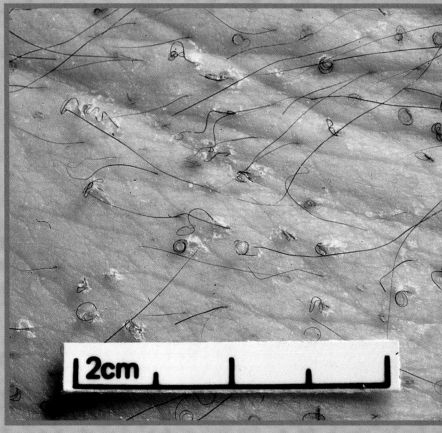

▲ *Corkscrew hairs on the skin of a patient suffering from scurvy.*

Timeline

1700s
Many sailors died
of scurvy at sea

1795
Lime juice carried
on all ships

1747
Dr James Lind carried
out an experiment on
12 sailors

1800s
Many scientific
advances made in
the field of medicine

1911
Vitamins discovered

1935
Vitamin C produced and
sold to the public

1931
Ascorbic acid (vitamin C)
identified in lemon juice

The News Today

FINALLY, THE TRUTH IS OUT!

Dr Lind's experiment in 1747 was the beginning of the search for vitamins.

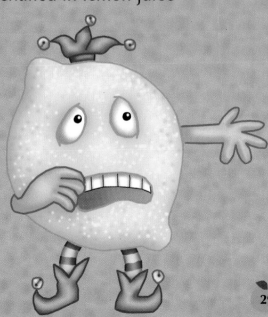

Glossary

acid a sour liquid

ascorbic acid the chemical name for vitamin C

cholera a very serious disease carried in dirty water or food. The patient is very sick and has diarrhoea

collagen a protein found in skin, bone, cartilage and tendon which acts as a glue, holding the body together

diet all the foods that we eat

deficiency lack or shortage

hypothesis   an idea used as the starting point for planning an experiment

navigator   sailor and explorer

symptom   a sign or feature of disease

smallpox   a very serious disease spread by the air or by touching someone who has the disease already. The patient has red spots full of pus.

vitamins   substances needed in small amounts in the diet to stay healthy. They are called vitamin A, B, C, D, E, K and M

Index